PICTURE A COUNTRY

Australia

Henry Pluckrose

W
FRANKLIN WATTS
NEW YORK • LONDON • SYDNEY

This is the Australian flag.

First published in 1999 by
Franklin Watts
96 Leonard Street
London
EC2A 4RH

Franklin Watts Australia
14 Mars Road
Lane Cove
NSW 2066

Copyright © Franklin Watts 1999

ISBN 0 7496 3330 1

Dewey Decimal Classification Number 919.4

A CIP catalogue record for this book is available from the British Library

Series editor: Rachel Cooke
Series designer: Kirstie Billingham
Editor: Alex Young
Picture research: Sue Mennell

Printed in Great Britain

Photographic acknowledgements:

Cover: Top right, Eye Ubiquitous (Grenville Turner/Wildlight Photo Agency), bottom left, Robert Harding Picture Library (D. Jacobs), bottom right (above), Bruce Coleman (Fritz Prenzel), bottom right (below), Window on the World (David Usill).

Insides: AA Photo Library p. 22, 23t, 23b; Bruce Coleman Collection pp. 8, 18 (Fritz Prenzel), 17b (Dr. Frieder Sauer); Colorific pp 12-13 (Bill Bachman), 16 (Patrick Ward), 20 (Penny Tweedie), 27 (Roger Garwood); James Davis Travel Photography p. 15; Eye Ubiquitous pp. 8-9 (Tony Brow Photography), 21 (Grenville Turner/Wildlight Photography), 28 (Paul Thompson); Getty Images p. 13 (Trevor Mein); Ronald Grant Archive p. 25b; Robert Harding Picture Library pp. 14 (D. Jacobs), 26 (Robert Francis), 29t; Image Bank p. 29b; Images Colour Library p.10; Impact Photos pp. 19 (Tom Webster), 24 (Neil Morrison); Christine Osborne Photos p. 25t; Spectrum Colour Library pp. 10-11; Window on the World Photo Library p. 17t (David Ustill).

All other photography Steve Shott.

Map by Julian Baker.

Contents

Where is Australia?

This is a map of Australia. Australia is a huge island south of Asia, in the Southern Hemisphere. Tasmania, a smaller island to the south-east of the mainland, is also part of Australia.

Here are some Australian stamps and money.

Australian money is counted in dollars.

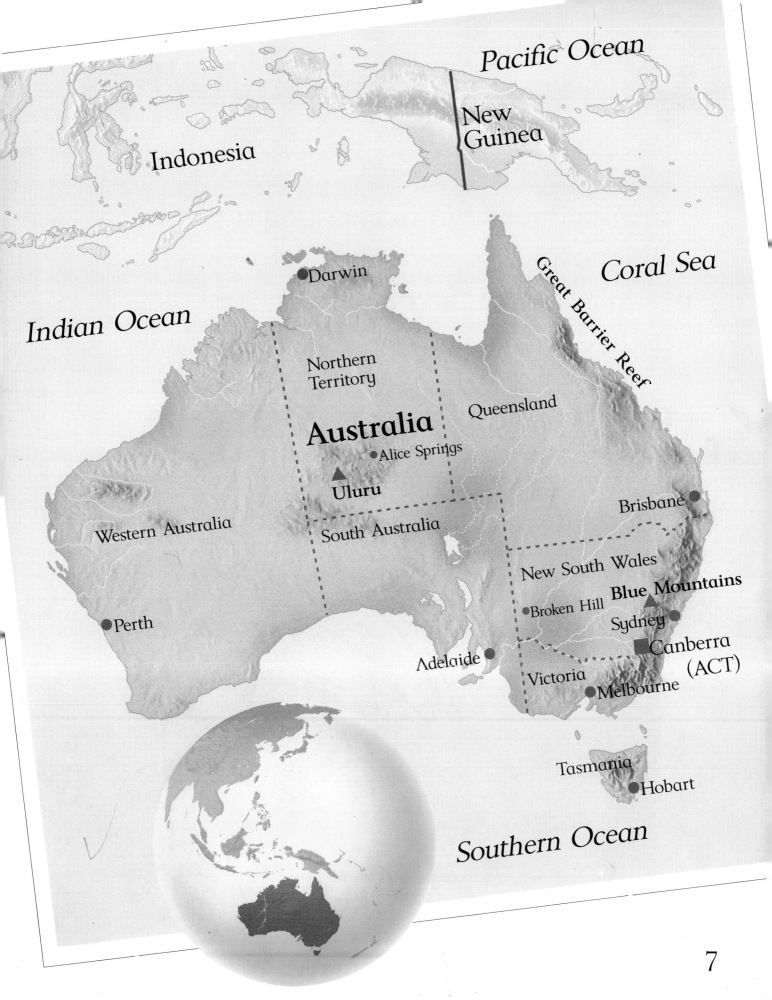

Pacific Ocean

Indonesia

New
Guinea

Indian Ocean

Coral Sea

Darwin

Northern
Territory

Great Barrier Reef

Australia

Queensland

Alice Springs

▲
Uluru

Western Australia

South Australia

Brisbane

New South Wales

Broken Hill

Blue Mountains
▲
Sydney

Perth

■ Canberra
(ACT)

Adelaide

Victoria

Melbourne

Tasmania

Hobart

Southern Ocean

7

The Australian landscape

Australia has many kinds of landscape. There are mountain ranges, tropical rainforests and green plains. But most of Australia is dry desert and scrub land, which stretches for many thousands of kilometres.

The desert regions of Australia are known as the Outback.

The peaks of the Three Sisters range are in the Blue Mountains in New South Wales.

Because Australia is in the Southern Hemisphere, its seasons are in the opposite order to countries north of the Equator. Summer is from December to February and winter from June to August.

The Australian people

The Aborigines are the native people of Australia. They first came to Australia over 40,000 years ago from islands in the Indian and Pacific Oceans.

When British people came to Australia in the 18th century, many Aborigines were made to leave their land.

Crowds gather to watch the famous Melbourne Cup horse race.

More than 18 million people live in Australia today. They have come from more than 200 different countries, including the UK, Ireland, Italy, Greece and several Asian countries.

Hobart is the capital of the island of Tasmania.

Where they live

Most Australians live in towns and cities along the south and east coasts, where the weather is rarely too hot or too cold. There are also many small towns in the Outback.

Nearly 3 million people live in Melbourne.

Capital cities

Australia is divided into different states and territories, each with its own capital. The state capitals are: Sydney (New South Wales), Adelaide (South Australia), Brisbane (Queensland), Perth (Western Australia), Melbourne (Victoria) and Hobart (Tasmania).

Sydney's Opera House is one of the most famous sights in Australia.

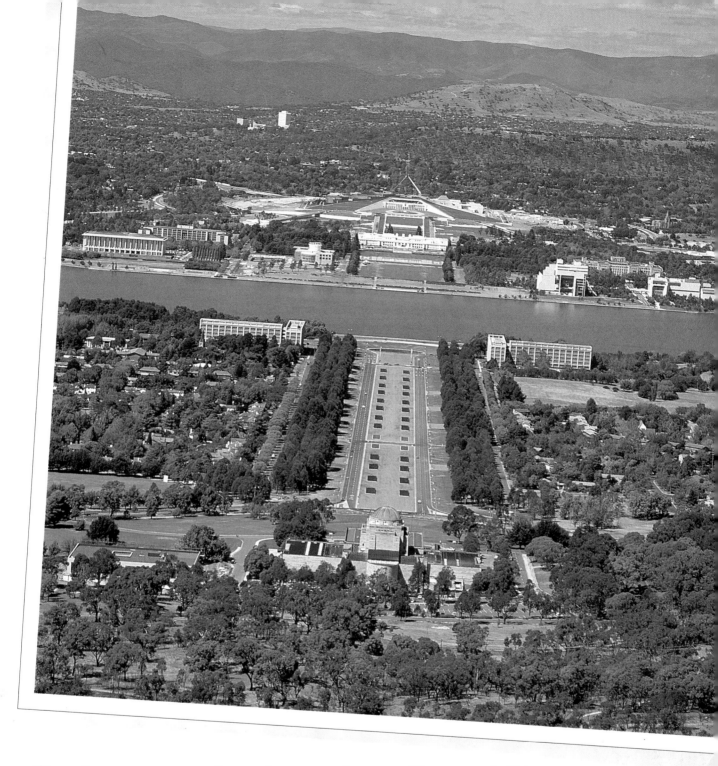

Canberra, in the Australian Capital Territory
(ACT), is the capital of the whole of
Australia. The most important building
in the city is the Parliament Building.

Diamonds and opals

Mining is important in Australia. Its rocks contain many precious stones, such as diamonds and opals. There are also valuable metals such as copper, silver and gold in the rocks, as well as oil and natural gas.

These miners are digging for opals by hand. It is hard and dangerous work.

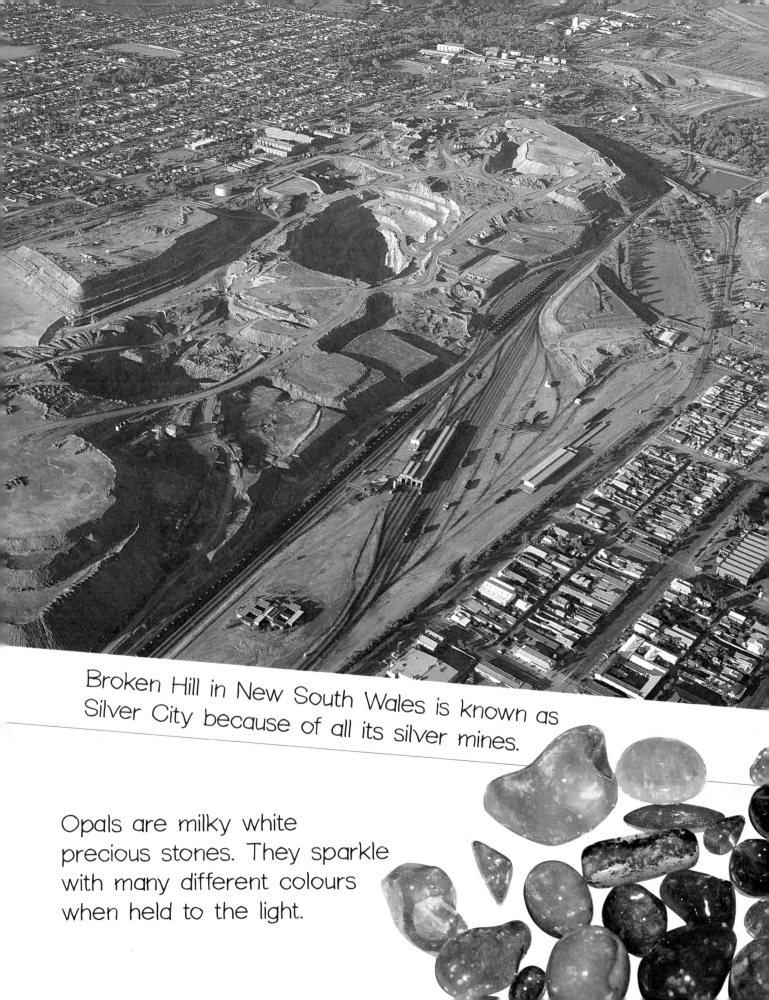

Broken Hill in New South Wales is known as Silver City because of all its silver mines.

Opals are milky white precious stones. They sparkle with many different colours when held to the light.

In Queensland, there is enough rain to grow all kinds of fruit and vegetables. This farm grows pineapples.

Farming

Where there is enough water, farmers grow wheat, fruit - such as pineapples - and vegetables. Only 70,000 people live and work in the dry Outback. Most of them raise cattle and sheep on huge farms called stations.

Farmers shear sheep for their wool and sell them for their meat.

The Outback

In the Outback, farms and small communities are very far apart. Life is very different for people living in these remote places.

The Flying Doctor Service began in Alice Springs in 1929. Alice Springs is in the middle of the Outback.

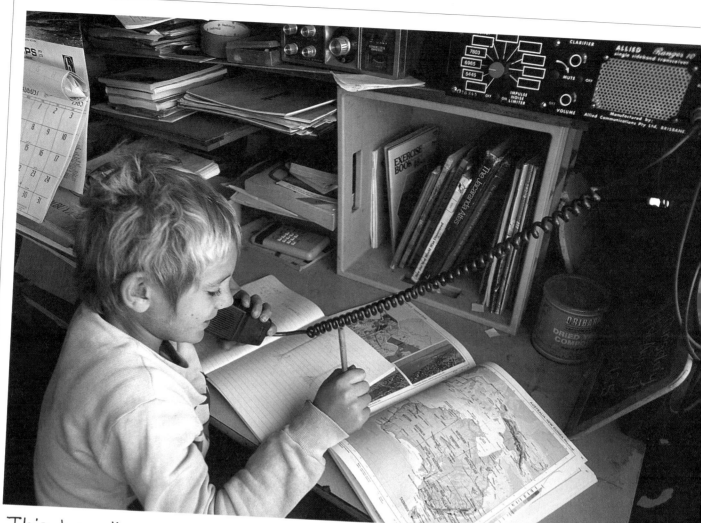

This boy lives a long way from a school, so he is learning geography over the radio.

Instead of going to school, children in the Outback have lessons by radio. This means they may never see their teachers! If people in the Outback are sick, the doctor comes to their house by plane or helicopter.

Australian food

Because so many different nationalities live in Australia, many types of food are eaten - from spicy Chinese dishes to sweet Greek pastries. Australians enjoy eating outdoors and often cook steaks, sausages and seafood on a barbecue.

The city of Melbourne has a large Greek population so many shops sell Greek food.

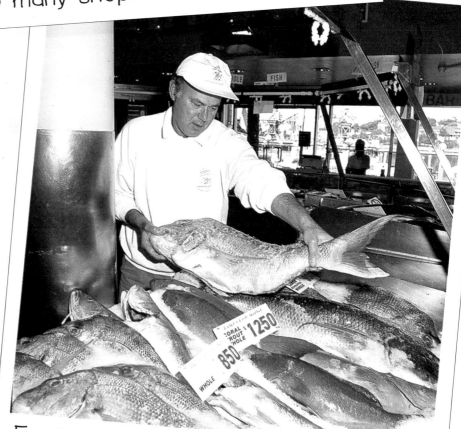

Fresh fish is sold in markets all along the Australian coast.

Out and about

Australians play all kinds of sport.
They enjoy rugby, cricket, tennis and golf.
Australia is also a great place for water sports.

Surfing is the most popular water sport in Australia.
The sea is warm and the waves can be very big.

This Aboriginal painting shows a snake and a bandicoot (a kind of rat).

Aboriginal artists are famous for their paintings. People go to see them in caves and in art galleries.

Australians also enjoy going to the cinema. Many successful films are made in Australia each year.

The popular film 'Babe' was made in Australia.

Festivals old and new

Australia's National Day is 26th January.
On Australia Day there are big parties
all around the country.

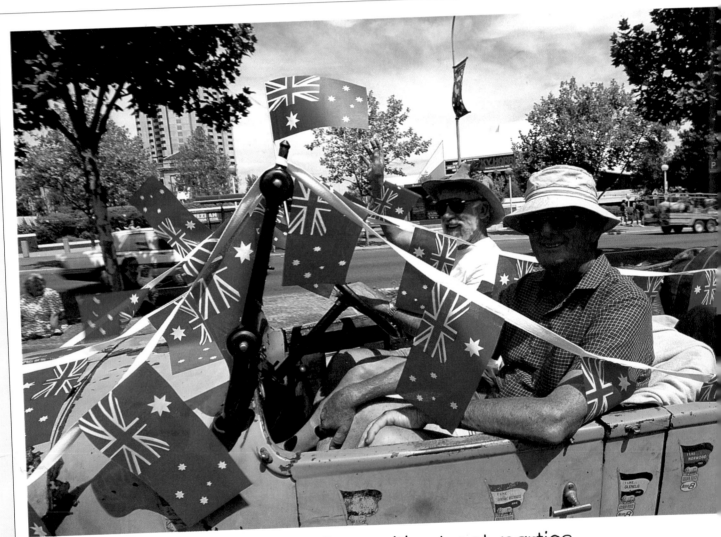

People celebrate Australia Day with street parties
and carnivals.

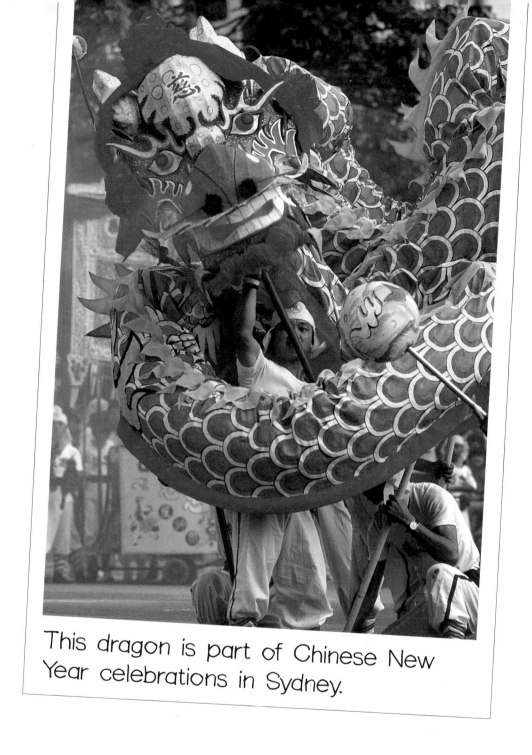

This dragon is part of Chinese New Year celebrations in Sydney.

Because people from so many different countries live in Australia, festivals, such as Chinese New Year and St. Patrick's Day, have become part of Australian life.

Visiting Australia

People visit Australia to see its amazing landscape, relax on its beautiful beaches and experience the excitement and adventure of the Outback.

Uluru stands in the middle of the desert. It is a religious site for Aboriginal people and its name means 'meeting place' in their language. Until recently Uluru was known as Ayers Rock.

Many tourists go diving in the coral of the Great Barrier Reef.

People also come to see Australia's strange animals, such as koalas, kangaroos, and the duck-billed platypus.

Index

About this book

The last decade of the 20th century has been marked by an explosion in communications technology. The effect of this revolution upon the young child should not be underestimated. The television set brings a cascade of ever-changing images from around the world into the home, but the information presented is only on the screen for a few moments before the programme moves on to consider some other issue.

Instant pictures, instant information do not easily satisfy young children's emotional and intellectual needs. Young children take time to assimilate knowledge, to relate what they already know to ideas and information which are new.

The books in this series seek to provide snapshots of everyday life in countries in different parts of the world. The images have been selected to encourage the young reader to look, to question, to talk. Unlike the TV picture, each page can be studied for as long as is necessary and subsequently returned to as a point of reference. For example, school life in the Outback might be compared with their own, or a discussion might develop about the ways in which food is prepared and eaten in a country whose culture and customs are different from their own.

The comparison of similarity and difference is the recurring theme in each of the titles in this series. People in different lands are superficially different. Where they live (the climate and terrain) obviously shapes the sort of houses that are built, but people across the world need shelter; coins may look different, but in each country people use money.

At a time when the world seems to be shrinking, it is important for children to be given the opportunity to focus upon those things which are common to all the peoples of the world. By exploring the themes touched upon in the book, children will begin to appreciate that there are strands in the everyday life of human beings which are universal.